Neighborhood Soup

A Play

Janet Stutley
Illustrated by Betty Greenhatch

The Characters

Kapi

Kapi's Mom

Kapi's Dad

Mr. Smith

Mrs. Jackson

Mr. Jackson

Uncle Sampat

Mom: Good news! Uncle Sampat is coming for dinner. Let's make his favorite vegetable soup.

Kapi: I like making soup!

Dad: I like eating soup!

(Mom and Dad look at a recipe book.)

Mom: We need a half cup
of chopped carrots.
One carrot is about
half a cup.

Dad: And we need one cup
of chopped potatoes.
I think two potatoes
will be enough.

Kapi: We need onions
and garlic, too.

Kapi: We need four cups of water. I'll put the water in the pot.

Mom: I'll chop the onions and garlic.

Dad: I'll chop the carrot and potatoes.

(Kapi looks at the recipe book.)

Kapi: We need one cup of beans.

Mom: Yes! And we need
one teaspoon of salt
and one tablespoon
of chopped basil.

Dad: The soup smells great already!

(Their neighbor, Mr. Smith, knocks at the door.)

Mom: Do you think Uncle Sampat

is here already?

Kapi: I'll see who it is.

(Kapi opens the door.)

Mr. Smith: Hello, Kapi.

Kapi: Hello, Mr. Smith! Come in.

Mr. Smith: I've brought you four tomatoes, fresh from my garden!

Mom: Thank you! Would you like to stay for dinner?

Kapi: We can put your tomatoes in the soup.

Dad: I'll just add a cup of water.

(Kapi's neighbors, Mr. and Mrs. Jackson, knock at the door. Kapi opens the door.)

Mrs. Jackson: Hello, Kapi. What are you cooking?

Mr. Jackson: It smells delicious!

Kapi: Hello, Mr. and Mrs. Jackson. We're making soup.

Mrs. Jackson: We've brought you some parsley from our garden.

Mr. Jackson: We've brought you some celery, too!

Dad: Thank you! Why don't you join us for dinner?

Kapi: We can put your parsley and celery in the soup.

Mom: I'll just add another
two cups of water.

Dad: Here's a bigger pot.

*(Uncle Sampat walks in. Everyone
smiles at him.)*

Uncle Sampat: Hello, everyone!

All: Hello, Sampat.

Uncle Sampat: I've brought some tasty bread to have with dinner.

Kapi: Thank you for the bread, Uncle Sampat. We can eat it with our soup.

Uncle Sampat: Are you making vegetable soup? That's my favorite!

Dad: Yes, we are. And our neighbors brought some of the ingredients.

Kapi: This vegetable soup is special, Uncle Sampat. It's "neighborhood soup"!